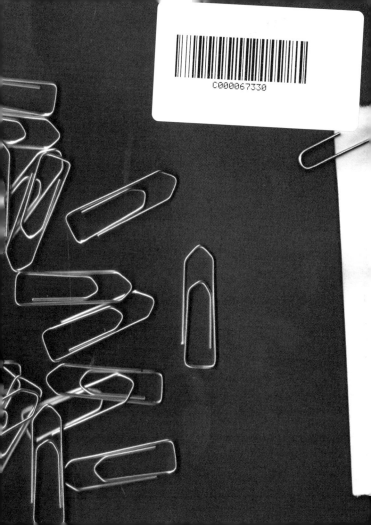

C000067330

First published 2018

ISBN: 978-1-910745-65-6

The paper used in this book is recyclable. It is made
from low chlorine pulps produced in a low energy,
low emissions manner from renewable forests.

Printed and bound by
Replika Press, Sonipat

Volume One

(Homo Sapiens
to
Damien Hirst)

Luath Press Limited

EDINBURGH

www.luath.co.uk

The author and publisher gratefully acknowledge the permission granted to reproduce the copyright material in this book.

Every effort has been made to trace copyright holders and to obtain their permission for the use of copyright material. The publisher apologises for any errors or omissions in the above list and would be grateful if notified of any corrections that should be incorporated in future reprints or editions of this book.

HOMO SAPIENS	40,000 BC
MICHELANGELO	1475–1564
REMBRANDT	1606–1669
FRAGONARD	1732–1806
GOYA	1746–1828
RUSKIN	1819–1900
CÉZANNE	1839–1906
VAN GOGH	1853–1890
SERGENT	1856–1925
NOLDE	1867–1956
PICASSO	1881–1973
DUCHAMP	1887–1968
SCHIELE	1890–1918
BOMBERG	1890–1957
GIACOMETTI	1901–1966
ROTHKO	1903–1970
DALÍ	1904–1989
POLLOCK	1912–1956
EARDLEY	1921–1963
FREUD	1922–2011
PAOLOZZI	1924–2005
HAMILTON FINLAY	1925–2006
LE WITT	1928–2007
ONO	1933–
HIRST	1965–

ART starts, as far as we know
not in the caves at Lascaux
  but with stencils of hands
  in all habited lands
HOMO SAPIENS saying 'Hallo!'

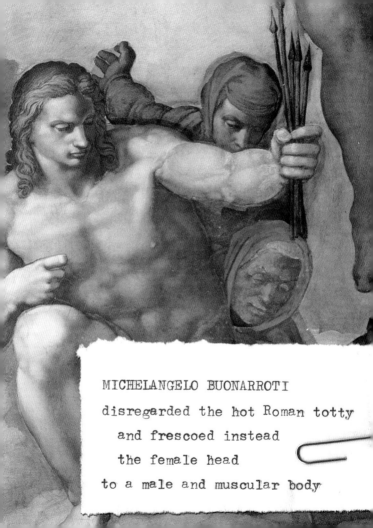

MICHELANGELO BUONARROTI

disregarded the hot Roman totty

and frescoed instead

the female head

to a male and muscular body

The self-portraits of REMBRANDT VAN RIJN
stare stoically out across time
  and I suppose
  in view of that nose
wondering... was it the wine?

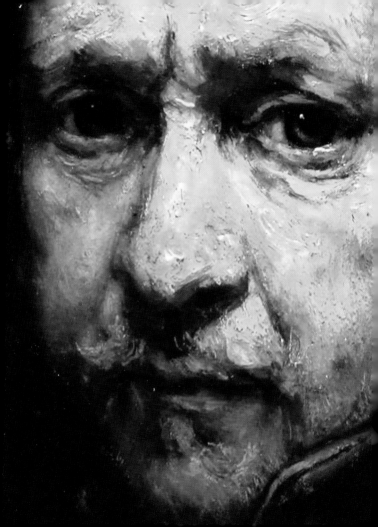

JEAN HONORE FRAGONARD!
Coquette on a swing! Ooh la la!
The whole court is lining up
'til they end climbing up
la Guillotine... Au revoir!

The mistress of FRANCISCO GOYA
was fun so he thought he'd employ her
to see if he'd dare
to depict pubic hair
and invite young Godoy to enjoy her

If through History of Art you are buskin'
and the state of your head needs adjustin'
   take a salutory dose
   of Victorian prose
try three days in bed with JOHN RUSKIN

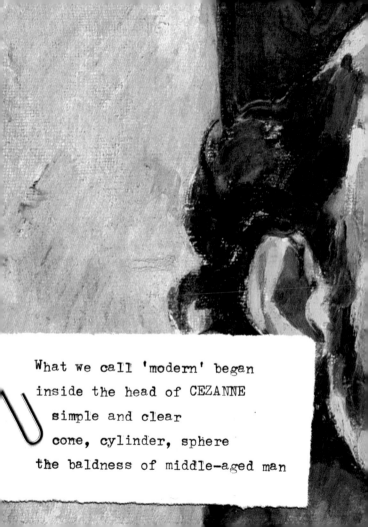

What we call 'modern' began
inside the head of CEZANNE
    simple and clear
    cone, cylinder, sphere
the baldness of middle-aged man

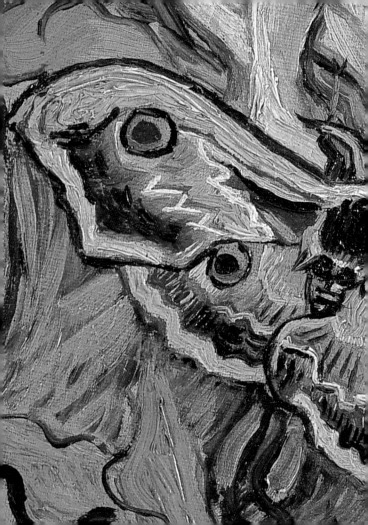

The unstoppable VINCENT VAN GOGH
switched on and then couldn't switch off
he says it with brio
in letters to Theo
he's drawn to the flame like a moth

Arch-flatterer JOHN SINGER SARGENT
was tops in the portrait department
  but never confessed
  about men he undressed
and drew in his private apartment

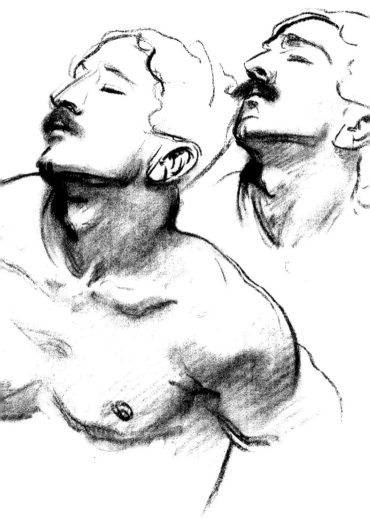

The German Expressionist **NOLDE**

was a chap with a chip on his shoulder

  Hitler said: 'Purge

  that degenerate splurge

and too bad he's a party card-holder!'

It's odd that in Burkina Faso
they pay tribute to PABLO PICASSO
the white-man who owed them
the mask and the totem
that took him from garret to chateau

PABLO RUIZ PICASSO 1881·1973

Science et Charité 1897

400F

REPUBLIQUE DE HAUTE-VOLTA

Somewhere in the arrière plan
of the mind-games of MARCEL DUCHAMP
you find him confessing
the point of cross-dressing
was Dada, and also maman

The shame (and the fame) would be SCHIELE's
the money all went to the dealers
   who saw the potential
   of skinny but sensual
in these Viennese Christine Keelers

There's an eloquent photo of BOMBERG
in a hat too askew to be somber
    he's looking at you
    as a working-class jew
with a taunt in the slant of his homberg

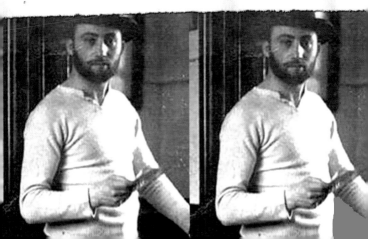

After the war GIACOMETTI
made figures with legs like spaghetti
    when asked to explain
    he said: 'In the main
it's consciously Samuel Beckett-y'

There's a room in the Tate where the goths go
where solitary men of the cloth know
   that there they can tune
   into Black on Maroon
and swoon in the gloom of a ROTHKO

The uncomfortable truth about DALI
was the choice he made politicali
    tout à fait surréelle
    but for Luis Bunuel
it mattered with whom you got pali

The drippings and pourings of POLLOCK
take liberties with the symbolic
    part Cherokee
    part painterly glee
part Long Island alcoholic

To list the achievement of **EARDLEY**
is a task that I undertake gleardly
there's houses with corbels
then kids in the Gorbals
with seascapes at Catterline, thirdly

I think I'd be rather annoyed
to be stared at by LUCIEN FREUD
    as though I were — ouch!
raw meat on the couch
uncounselled, and facing the void

Consider the magpie PAOLOZZI
who sees all of art as his proxy
    confronting a classic
    he'll take it and smash it
then glue it back up with epoxy

In the garden of HAMILTON FINLAY
is a god that we apprehend dimly
  in a pastoral hollow
  a golden Apollo
has a stare with a hint of the Hindley

The obsessive compulsive LEWITT
will cover your walls bit by bit
with millions of lines
but nobody minds
because he just HAS to do it

She's mother-of-all YOKO ONO
of Geldof & Bowie & Bono
who now never cease
to bang on about peace
tho I'm guessing the bed-in's a no-no

The method of DAMIEN HIRST
is to get the title done first
  it has to be catchy
  to get through to Saatchi
and thus is the market coerced

It's good to have a title
that's not just one word.
If you're gonna title it
you might as well try
and say something.

Damien Hirst

Notes

Homo Sapiens 40,000 BC

Astonishingly, some 100,000 years after the appearance of HOMO SAPIENS, all separate groups of this species leave near identical markings in the caves they inhabit across the planet. The earliest known paintings are in Indonesia and predate those in Lascaux by a whopping 22,700 years. The handprints in the image are from the Cueva de las Manos (Cave of the Hands) in the Santa Cruz province in Argentina.

Photograph by Mariano, 2005; reproduced courtesy of Wiki commons.com

Michelangelo 1475–1564

Jumping swiftly forward to the greatest decorated cave of the 16th century, the image shows St Catherine beside an unusually muscular St Sebastian, as depicted on the altar wall of the Sistine Chapel in Rome. But not exactly. For MICHELANGELO, pioneer of the iconic muscular Christian martyr, she was naked. It took all 18 years (and three popes' worth) of the Council of Trent, the long-drawn-out response of the Catholic church to Protestantism, for Pius IV finally to instruct Daniele da Volterra to hide the nakedness. So, in terms of the Last Judgement, it's a case of model by Michelangelo, clothes by Volterra.

Image courtesy of Wiki commons.com

Rembrandt 1606–1669

REMBRANDT went bust in 1656, and the inventory of his possessions included none of the 50 or so self-portraits that he painted throughout his career. In other words, he didn't paint them for himself as Romantic interrogations of the creative act, but because he could sell them. In the opinion of Hans-Joachim Raupp he '… *did not step into the mirror with questions and doubts, but with a carefully planned programme.*'[1] The art-buying public collected images – and particularly head and shoulder studies – of famous people. The self-portrait was an opportunity to feed

1 Susan Fegley Osmond, 'Rembrandt's Self-Portraits' *The Mind and I* Magazine, Washington, 2000.

this taste, to paint from a free model, and to showcase his unusual technique. This portrait 'with beret and turned-up collar' is from 1659, and is in the National Gallery of Art, Washington DC.

Image courtesy of Wiki commons.com

Fragonard   1732–1806

Darling of the court of Louis XV and XVI, the great Rococo master FRAGONARD fell completely from view for more than a century following the French Revolution and the beheading of his erstwhile patrons. However, in happier days of pre-revolutionary 1767 he painted *Les Hasards Heureux de l'Escarpolette*, or *The Happy Accidents of the Swing*. She tosses a slipper to her concealed lover, while her unwitting husband provides the momentum.

In the Wallace Collection, London; reproduced courtesy of Wiki commons.com

Goya   1746–1828

GOYA, well known for his graphic depictions of war and nightmare, was also a pioneering erotic artist and, it seems, the first to paint a nude (with pubic hair) who was an actual woman rather than the template for a goddess. *La Maja Desnuda* was hung in a chamber behind an identical image of the same woman clothed, in private rooms designed for the purpose by Manuel Godoy y Álvarez de Faria, then Prime Minister of Spain. Both Goya and Godoy (the younger man) were lovers of this feisty and daring Spanish beauty, whose identity is still contested.

circa 1795, in the Prado Museum, Madrid; reproduced courtesy of Wiki commons.com

Ruskin   1819–1900

For the aesthete RUSKIN, 60 years later, pubic hair was still a surprise. Married to Effie Gray in 1848, the marriage remained unconsummated and was annulled in 1854. In picky and prudish prose Ruskin rationalised the reason: '... *though her face was beautiful, her person was not formed to excite passion. On the contrary, there were certain circumstances in her person which completely checked it...*'.[2] A lesson or two from Goya might have been in order on this score, but nevertheless

---

2   Lutyens, M., *Millais and the Ruskins*, London: John Murray, 1967, p.191.

should not diminish his remarkable contribution as art critic, patron, social philosopher, environmentalist etc etc.

Cézanne   1839–1906

CÉZANNE, on the other hand, remains unabashed not so much by the presence of hair, as the lack of it. Like Rembrandt he left many self-portraits that depict both progressive hair-loss, and the progressively analytical detachment that became his creed. He sums it up in 1904 in a letter to his protégé Émile Bernard: '... *treat nature by means of the cylinder, the sphere, the cone, everything brought into proper perspective so that each side of an object or plane is directed towards a central point*...'.[3] The letter is regarded as marking the end of the Impressionist period in French art.

Van Gogh   1853–1890

Émile Bernard was also the recipient of letters and advice from VINCENT VAN GOGH, although the vast bulk, including the unsent last letter found in his breast pocket, were addressed to his brother Theo. The threads of writing, drawing and painting weave together throughout Van Gogh's career, informing, provoking and sustaining one another. A favourite metaphor for self-transformation, both pictorial and literary, was the metamorphosis of the butterfly as a symbol of hope. However, by May 1889 Van Gogh had committed himself to the care of Dr Gachet in the asylum at Saint-Rémy, where, after a series of butterfly paintings he portrayed this remarkable (and nocturnal) Green Peacock moth. What does it mean? Strangely, the painting is known as the 'Emperor Moth' in the Van Gogh museum, but was titled by Van Gogh himself as 'Death's Head Moth'.

---

3   Paul Cézanne, Letter to Emile Bernard, 15 April 1904.

Sargent

Under the questionable pretext of making studies for biblical compositions, such as '*David in Saul's Camp*' and '*The Sorrowful Mysteries*', the esteemed society portraitist JOHN SINGER SARGENT compiled a large and completely private folio of extravagantly posed naked men, frequently (as in this sketch) with bound arms. For models he chose languid gondoliers (see: *Head of a Gondolier*, 1880), his magnificently moustached manservant Nicola d'Iverno, and Thomas McKeller, (see: *Portrait*, 1917) whom he met in a lift in Boston. This obsession spans his entire career, outliving his other portrait work from which he retired in 1907 with the excuse that he could no longer tolerate the small-talk.

'Sketch for the Sorrowful Mysteries, The Carrying of the Cross – Head and Shoulders of a Man' Museum of Fine Arts, Boston, circa 1900; reproduced courtesy of Wiki commons.com

Nolde

When EMIL NOLDE joined the Nazi Party in 1934 he was already 67 years old and should have known better. He was, however, keen to be seen as the pre-eminent modern German artist of the new ideology of a racially pure Volk. He tried to distinguish his expressionism from that of other similar painters, falsely denouncing his colleague Max Pechstein as Jewish, and choosing completely different subject matter. Unlike both his contemporaries and his hero Van Gogh, he avoided any subject matter that smacked of social critique or socialist sympathy. He was admired and collected by both Speer and Goebbels, but even these leading Nazis could not sway the inflexibly neo-classical taste of their Führer. Nolde's work was included in the 'Degenerate Art' exhibition in Berlin in 1938 (about which he protested vociferously) and he was banned from artistic activity in 1941. The image shows his erstwhile patron Goebbels, with attendant SS officers, striding – appropriately enough – past Nolde's depiction of *Christ and the Sinner*.

Image courtesy of the German Federal Archive, reproduced courtesy of Wiki commons.com

Picasso

It is well known that PICASSO fished around in French colonial plunder for inspiration. Led on by Matisse, he conquered his revulsion at the

Trocadero Museum and discovered instead, among the piles of artefacts: '… *what painting really meant… it's a form of magic that interposes itself between us and a hostile universe… a means of seizing power by imposing a form on our terrors…*'[4] All of which amounts to a complex rationalisation of the colonial gaze. But what of the colonised? When these commemorative stamps were issued in sub-Saharan former French colony Upper Volta to celebrate the 10th anniversary of Picasso's death, Picasso's primitivism (to say nothing of his cubist, blue, rose, neo-classicist, surrealist or expressionist periods) was entirely ignored, and his status as an artist recognised only in works that Picasso had already achieved by the age of 16. They are an early self-portrait, a portrait of his mother, the image '1st communion' and a deathbed scene entitled 'Science and Charity'. And such-like *European* forms of magic. The stamps were issued in 1983 in the country that would become Burkina Faso later that year, following Thomas Sankara's revolution.

Photograph by Angus Reid from his own stamp collection.

Duchamp   1887–1968

Avant-guardist MARCEL DUCHAMP, always ahead of the game, was the first artist to depict himself as a transvestite, with a typically punning alias. One phonetic rearrangement of the syllables Mar-cel-Du-champ is mar-chand-du-sel, meaning 'salt merchant', a fitting and witty dig at Duchamp invented by another irrepressible punster, the French Surrealist poet Robert Desnos in the collection he wrote in homage to Duchamp's alter ego, Rrose Sélavy.

Rrose Sélavy (Marcel Duchamp) 1921 Photograph by Man Ray, Art Direction by Marcel Duchamp. Philadelphia Museum of Art, reproduced courtesy of Wiki commons.com

Schiele   1890–1918

The good citizens of Vienna, Český Krumlov and Neulengbach all failed to lock up their daughters when EGON SCHIELE came to town and, misconstruing his art as pornography, either hounded him out or prosecuted and imprisoned him. None of which put Schiele off, whose depictions of female sexuality became increasingly explicit, culminating

4   Andrew Meldrum, 'How much did Picasso's paintings borrow from African Art?' *The Guardian*, 15 March 2006.

in the masturbation portraits of 1918. The Viennese dealer cited in the limerick is Rudolph Leopold, who refused to exhibit or sell the short-lived Schiele's paintings, but who was more than happy to buy them, amassing the largest collection of his work in the world. It was an astute move, as all the work was eventually bought by the Austrian government and the National Bank of Austria, and exhibited in the Leopold museum, of which the long-lived Rudolph was made first director.

Woman with green stockings, 1917 Private collection, reproduced courtesy of Wiki commons.com

Bomberg   1890–1957

If there is proof that social mobility is the engine of innovation in art, it is surely exemplified by DAVID BOMBERG. The seventh of eleven children of an East End working class migrant family, Bomberg's ferocious talent got him into the Slade School, and then expelled for unrepentant Futurism. The photograph is from 1925, after his devastating experience as a private soldier in the trenches of the Western Front, and in the course of his self-appointed mission to re-envision the landscape and the figure. At this time he produced his landscapes in Palestine. In 1933, briefly, he became a member of the communist party. His background, his Jewishness and his socialism alienated him from the British establishment for his entire life, a haughty disdain from which his achievements as a draughtsman, painter and teacher have only recently re-remerged.

Image courtesy of Wiki commons.com

Giacometti   1901–1966

GIACOMETTI's distinctive style emerged at the same time and in the same place as Beckett's mature drama: post-war Paris. The two artists had known one another for 20 years and Giacometti expressed dissatisfaction with the set-design of the first production of *Waiting for Godot*. In 1961, for a new production of *Godot* at the Théâtre de l'Odéon, Beckett asked Giacometti to design the set, and the two men spent a night in late April creating the tree together. '*We spent the whole night in the studio with that plaster tree,*' Giacometti recalled, '*trying to make it sparser, smaller, the branches thinner. It never looked any good and neither he nor I liked it…*'.[5] The design was a success, and the template for the alien landscapes in which all Beckett's future drama would be set. Asked later to comment on the relationship between the arts, the curmudgeonly Beckett retorted that he had '*… never felt that painting or sculpture can express the same things as literature. I don't see any parallel between the two arts.*'[6] For me, however, the common vision is eerily foreseen in a line by the British war poet Keith Douglas: '*I see men as trees, suffering*'.[7]

Image reproduced by kind permission of the Fondation Alberto et Annette Giacometti © Succession Alberto Giacometti (Fondation Alberto et Annette Giacometti + ADAGP) Paris

Rothko   1903–1970

In 1958 MARK ROTHKO described, in an admirably candid lecture to the Pratt Institute, the 'recipe' of a work of art. The ingredients are:

1. Death
2. Sensuality
3. Tension
4. Irony
5. Play
6. Chance
7. Hope

He went on: '*I measure these ingredients very carefully when I paint a picture. The picture results from the proportions of these elements.*'[8] Commissioned to make paintings for the vast Seagram Restaurant in New York he stated that he '*… hoped to ruin the appetite of every son-of-a-bitch who ever eats in that room*'.[9] These are the paintings that are now on display at the Tate Gallery in London.

Photograph by Dinda Fass, 2016; reproduced courtesy of the artist.

5   Quoted in Hohl, *Giacometti: A Biography with Pictures*, Gerd Hatje, Ostfildern, 1998, p.169.
6   Lord, *Some Remarkable Men, Further Memoirs*, Farrar Strauss Giroux, New York, 1996, p.289.
7   Desmond Graham, *Keith Douglas – a biography*, OUP 1974, p188. The poem is titled 'Desert Flowers'.
8   Mark Rothko, Lecture to the Pratt Institute, 1947.
9   Conversation with John Fischer, published *Harper's* magazine, 1970.

Dalí

SALVADOR DALÍ chose not to condemn the fascist movements of the '30s, and was expelled from the Surrealist movement for this reason in 1934. Fascinated by the dream-like possibilities of film, he had collaborated with Luis Buñuel on *Un Chien Andalou*, and *L'Age d'Or*, but Dalí's political position spelled the end of their joint endeavours. During the Spanish Civil War Buñuel gave his services to the Republican side, making *España 1936*, and *España leal ¡en armas!*; Dalí on the other hand continued to flirt with right-wing aristocrats and indulge a shared fascination for Hitler, famously stating that he '*liked to imagine Hitler as a woman…*'. Despite his long life he never repented, and this remarkable photograph is from 1972. Dalí has depicted the Spanish dictator Franco's grand-daughter as the personification of Spain. He is presenting the painting to Franco, along with his daughter and grand-daughter Carmen Martinez Bordiu. As George Orwell put it: '*One ought to be able to hold in one's head simultaneously the two facts that Dali is a good draughtsman and a disgusting human being*'.[10]

Attribution: unknown.

Pollock

The cost of reproducing not only a painting but even a simple portrait photograph of JACKSON POLLOCK is beyond the reach of this modest volume. However, it is fortunate that Pollock's work extends beyond the image library, and beyond the canvas itself. The photograph shows *the studio floor* used by Jackson Pollock at the Pollock-Krasner House in Springs, New York. Pollock put a wood floor down and used it as his primary painting surface from 1946 until his death in 1956, the period of his best-known work. However, Pollock's alcoholism eventually undid him. On an August night in 1956, despite being cautioned by the police, Pollock drove on recklessly, killing himself and a friend Edith Metzger, and badly injuring his mistress, Ruth Kligman.

Photograph by Rhododendrites, 2015, reproduced courtesy of Wiki commons.com

---

10 George Orwell, '*Benefit of Clergy – some notes on Salvador Dali*', in Critical Essays, Secker and Warburg, London 1946.

Eardley

JOAN EARDLEY died at 42 – appallingly young – but still ten years older than Sylvia Plath, her direct contemporary. They died in the same year, and it is unlikely that Eardley knew of Plath, or vice versa. Nevertheless, to me at least, they are sisters in spirit in their joint interrogation of the elemental forces of landscape and the fragile mishmash of influences that make up human identity. This beautiful photograph of Eardley at work in Catterline was taken by her life-long admirer, Audrey Walker.

Photograph by Audrey Walker, reproduced courtesy of The Scottish Gallery, Edinburgh.

Freud

LUCIAN FREUD never forgot himself to be the grandson of Sigmund Freud, the father of psychoanalysis. For a prose version of my limerick see Professor Edward Chaney's description of Freud's method: '… *the distinctive recumbent manner in which Freud poses so many of his sitters suggest the conscious influence of his grandfather's psychoanalytic couch… his dreaming figures, staring into space until (if ever) brought back to health…*'.[11] When, however, the couch is a place to be observed rather than healed, the therapeutic aim of psychoanalysis is displaced by the materiality of the image. And the purpose of the material image is to be sold. At the time, Freud's '*Benefits Supervisor Sleeping*' was the most expensive painting ever sold by a living artist, making $33.6 million in 2008. In 2015, four years after his death, '*Benefits Supervisor Resting*' sold for $56.2 million.

Photograph by Jane Bown, reproduced courtesy of *The Guardian*.

Paolozzi

For EDUARDO PAOLOZZI – born in Edinburgh and locked up in Saughton prison as a 16 year old in 1940 for being Italian – rebellion against oppressive institutions came naturally. This included the institutions of Art and Art History. With his seminal collage *I Was A Rich Man's Plaything* both he and the nascent Pop Art movement set out to destroy them. He is the sculptor as vandal, hammer in hand, and his

---

11 Edward Chaney, 'Freudian Egypt', *The London Magazine* (April/May 2006), pp.62–69.

Michelangelo's David (1987), pictured in this book, celebrates the smashing of hated classical plaster-casts, the like of which he was obliged to draw at art college in Edinburgh in 1946, and which were pulverised during student riots in Munich in 1972.

Photograph by Repton1x, 2012, reproduced courtesy of Wiki commons.com

Hamilton Finlay   1925–2006

Scottish artist IAN HAMILTON FINLAY took the British obsession with all things Second World War to unparalleled aesthetic heights, and remains a deeply disconcerting artist, fetishizing the violence of wars and revolutions past. A concrete poet, '… *he fills his stanzas / With stenguns and panzas*',[12] not to mention battleships, landmines, ss insignia and guillotines, and surveys them all from a garden both actual and ideological. Actual in the sense that it exists at Little Sparta in the Pentland Hills; and ideological in the sense of Saint-Just: as the nature that persists after the death of the King and the Christian God. Saint-Just himself, the French revolutionary, is one of the beautiful male models for Finlay's merciless Apollo, and one architect of the terror in 'terroriste'.

Photograph by Murdo Macleod, reproduced courtesy of the photographer.

LeWitt   1928–2007

SOL LEWITT, despite dying in 2007, is remarkable for having achieved immortality. Credited for creating the Conceptualist movement, his ongoing work is best exemplified by the guidelines for installations and wall drawings of which LeWitt made many thousands, and which continue to be followed to this day. The *concept* – of which he is the author – is that the idea laid down in the guidelines surpasses the singular hand of the artist, and surpasses each work itself. A typical guideline might be: '*Within 4 adjacent squares, each 4' x 4', 4 draftsmen will be employed at $4 an hour for 4 hours per day for 4 days to draw straight lines 4" long using 4 different coloured pencils…*'.[13]

The image shows the creation of Wall Drawing 960 at Site Gallery Sheffield in 2010. Attribution: unknown.

12 Angus Reid, 1st draft of the IHF limerick, quoted so as not to waste a good rhyme, 2016.

13 Sol Lewitt, 'proposal for wall drawing', provenance unknown.

When on Valentine's Day 2003 Andrew and Christine Gale were holding a bed-in to protest against the looming Iraqi war in their own bedroom in Addingham, West Yorkshire, the phone rang and a voice offered sisterly support. It was YOKO ONO of John Lennon and the 1969 Amsterdam Hilton bed-in fame. The image in this book was taken in the immediate aftermath of the event, at an impromptu press-conference at Schipol Airport. The film of the sister event, the 1969 Montreal bed-in re-run BED PEACE, can be seen on YouTube with a message from Yoko Ono, and ends with an excellent montage of Instant Karma. John Lennon once described Yoko Ono as *the world's most famous unknown artist: everyone knows her name, but no one knows what she actually does*', which is unfair. The artist Yoko Ono has been campaigning for peace and human rights since the 1960s, and she rationalised her attitude to celebrity in a 2008 interview as '*I decided to love all the people who miss John*'. Which gets my vote.

Photograph by Marcela Cataldi Cipolla, reproduced courtesy of Wiki commons.com

Hirst   1965–

For the garrulous DAMIEN HIRST, art is simply 'a manipulative joke and a conduit to money'.[14] Now Britain's wealthiest artist (as well as one of its most bracingly candid) he grew up in Bristol and Leeds in a poor single parent family and left school with a single qualification: an 'E' at A-level Art. In the opinion of the critic Robert Hughes, Hirst represents the fact that today, financial value is the only meaning that remains for art. Hirst is eloquent on the subject of titles: 'Art goes on in your head. If you said something interesting, that might be the title for a work of art... I've always got a massive list of titles...'.[15] *Beautiful Inside My Head Forever* is the mystifying title of an inspired 2008 art-piece that took the form of an auction at Sotheby's, London, raising £111 million.

Quotation can be found at www.QuoteHD.com

---

14 Miles Richmond, *Imagination*, 10 October 2001.
15 'I knew it was time to clean up my act', *Daily Telegraph*, 26 July 2004.

THANK YOU — Karel, Dinda, Ken
and the late Alastair Mowat